The UNICORN ALPHABET

by MARIANNA MAYER
pictures by MICHAEL HAGUE

Dial Books · New York

For Lilli Scott with love   M.M.

To the Harts   M.H.

Published by Dial Books
A Division of Penguin Books USA Inc.
2 Park Avenue
New York, New York 10016

Published simultaneously in Canada
by Fitzhenry & Whiteside Limited, Toronto
Text copyright ©1989 by Marianna Mayer
Pictures copyright ©1989 by Michael Hague
All rights reserved
Typography by Nancy R. Leo
Printed in the U.S.A.
W
1 3 5 7 9 10 8 6 4 2

Library of Congress Cataloging in Publication Data

Mayer, Marianna/The unicorn alphabet.

Summary/The classic medieval legend of the unicorn
serves as a motif for the alphabet.
1. English language—Alphabet—Juvenile literature.
2. Unicorns—Juvenile literature.
[1. Unicorns. 2. Alphabet.]
I. Hague, Michael, ill. II. Title.
PE1155.M378 1989   [E]   86-13506
ISBN 0-8037-0372-4
ISBN 0-8037-0373-2 (lib. bdg.)

The art for each picture consists of a pen and ink,
watercolor, and gouache painting that is color-separated
and reproduced in full color.

THE UNICORN, a fabulous and beautiful animal, appears in ancient folklore in many cultures. He has been portrayed in art throughout the ages as either fierce and courageous or gentle and pure, but he is always magnificent. The medieval Unicorn Tapestries are some of the most superb examples of the unicorn myth; its hunt, capture, death, and resurrection are all depicted in a rich series of scenes. When these tapestries were designed, myth and symbolism were as real to people as everyday life. In the agrarian society in which they lived there was much lore and solemn belief surrounding all plants and animals. Medieval gardens were a source not only of nourishment and fragrance, but medicine as well, and many of these same plants were grown to ward off evil.

Plant and animal mythology was believed in so completely that the decorative motifs within the Unicorn Tapestries held important messages for viewers, and these symbols emphasized the meaning of the story more fully. As we come to understand each symbol, we see tales within tales that expand our appreciation. From the placement of the smallest violet to the tallest oak tree, each detail in a scene intensifies the story the tapestries set out to tell us.

There is virtually an alphabet from A to Z of the legend and lore of the unicorn. *The Unicorn Alphabet* draws on these stories and symbols as a tribute to the one-horned mythic beast and captures a glimpse of the beliefs of an earlier time.

MARIANNA MAYER

A · The *apple* is the fruit of autumn. In the Garden of Eden, Adam and Eve believed the apple was the fruit of knowledge. Like the unicorn, it is the symbol of ever-renewing life.

B · The *bluebell* is a small, delicate flower, but a tiny sprig was thought to protect against evil. In medieval times peasants hung the bluebell over their doorway to guard against mischievous spirits.

C · The slim *columbine* is an ancient flower. The medieval French considered it the flower of loyalty and constancy — qualities also given to the unicorn. Long ago the columbine was used in magic spells and as a remedy against poison.

D · The *daffodil* — flower, stem, and root — was once carried into battle by medieval knights who believed that the crushed root, laid upon a wound, would stop bleeding. The horn of the unicorn was believed to heal in the same way.

E · The *ermine* is a small, lithe animal whose dark fur turns snow-white in winter. In the Middle Ages the white ermine and the unicorn were both symbols of a maiden's purity.

F · The *fountain* was once the symbol of everlasting life and miraculous happenings. Legend tells of the waters from the fountain which feed a lake where all the good animals gathered to drink. There the unicorn watched over them.

G · The *goldfinch* sings her sweet song close to the unicorn. Though one of the smallest of birds, the goldfinch is the symbol of perseverance because she plucks ripe berries from among sharp thorns to feed herself and her young.

H · The *holly tree* was once a talisman and, like the unicorn's horn, a weapon against evil. With its pointed green leaves and bright red berries, holly was planted during the Middle Ages to protect against evil magic.

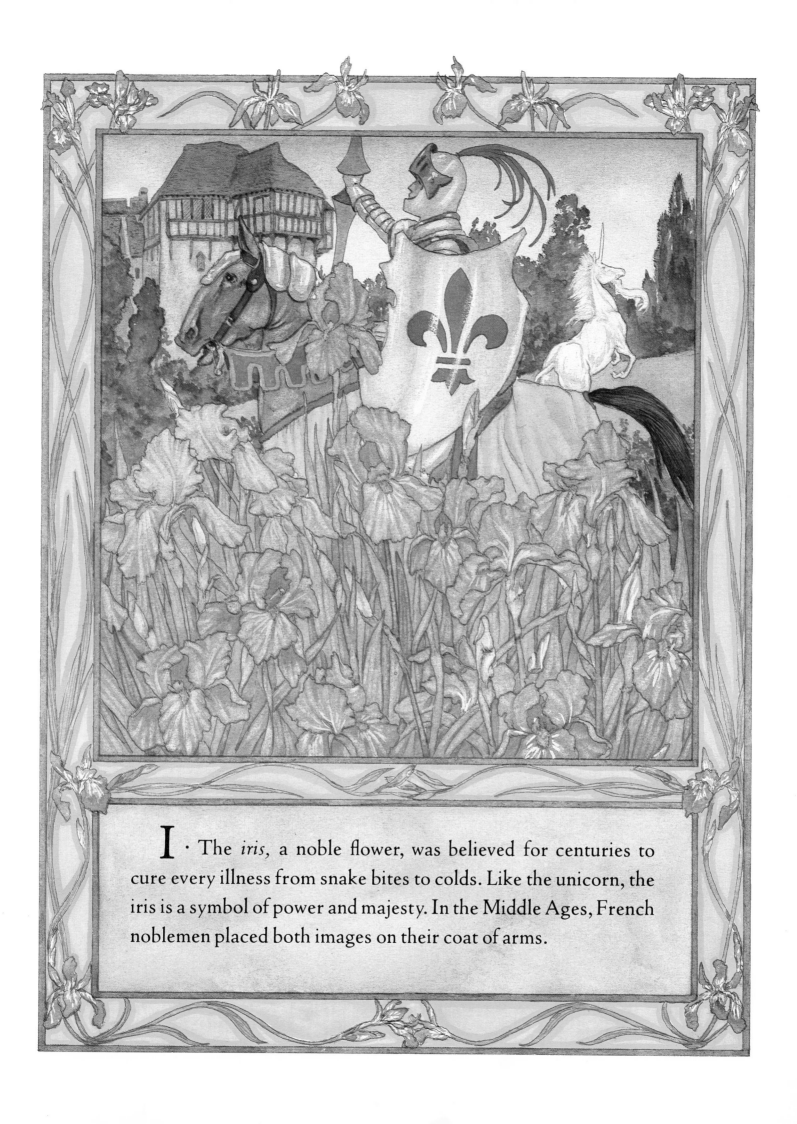

I · The *iris,* a noble flower, was believed for centuries to cure every illness from snake bites to colds. Like the unicorn, the iris is a symbol of power and majesty. In the Middle Ages, French noblemen placed both images on their coat of arms.

J· The *jewelweed* is a wild, flowering plant with small orange blossoms. Herbalists in ancient times used the milk-white juice from its stem to soothe the pain caused by poison ivy and the sting of prickly nettle plants.

K · The *Knight of the Unicorn* was the ideal medieval hero. In ballads and romances he was compared to the noble unicorn. Fierce and courageous, this knight fought against evil and yet had compassion for all defenseless creatures.

L · The tale of the *Lady of the Unicorn* was a popular ballad in medieval times. She was the symbol of virtue, often pictured riding a snow-white unicorn. Her true love was the Knight of the Lion, who fought against evil with his faithful lion at his side.

M · *Marigolds* and *mistletoe* have both been linked to the magnificent unicorn. Marigolds were gathered to cure snakebites and the mistletoe had medicinal uses, which are still considered to be effective today.

N · The *narwhal* is a small Arctic whale with a long, spi-
raled ivory horn. His horn is so like the unicorn's that it too was
used to cure ills. Medieval kings considered both a great treasure
to possess.

O · The *orange tree* and its bright fruit signify fertility. After the crusaders brought the orange from the Holy Land, medieval Europeans adopted the belief that it, like the unicorn, represented the sacred union between a bride and groom.

P · The *pomegranate* is the preeminent symbol of fertility. Medieval art often portrays the unicorn beside a pomegranate tree. A branch was believed to keep away snakes, and the ruby-red juice from its seeds healed the sting of the scorpion.

Q · In the *quest* for the unicorn medieval hunters were determined to gain his magical horn. Although all such quests ended in failure, today the myth of the unicorn still fascinates us.

R · The *rose* was the best-loved of all medieval flowers. Both the rose and the unicorn were adopted as allegorical symbols in medieval tales of love. Together and apart they represent betrothal and faithfulness in marriage.

S · The *serpent* was the enemy of the unicorn. In medieval myth the serpent lives near a lake where the animals come to drink. If not for the protection of the unicorn, the animals would be prey to the wily serpent.

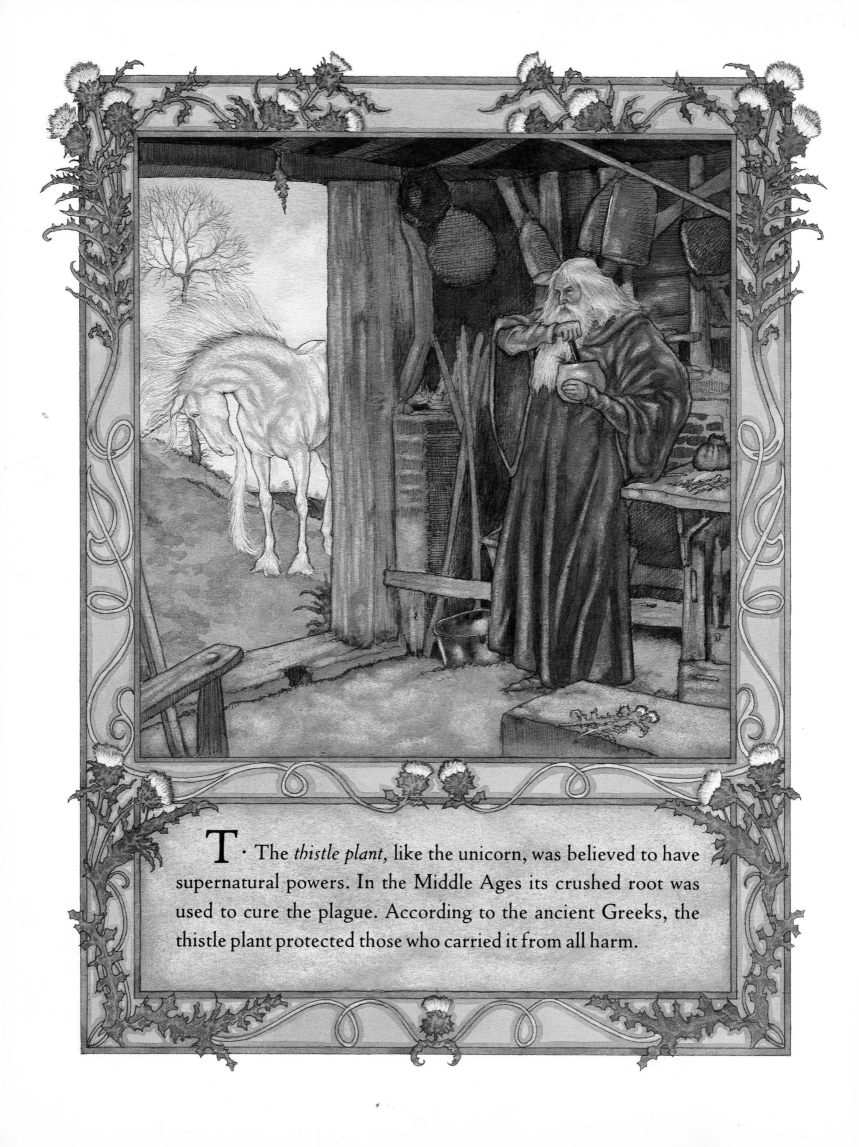

T· The *thistle plant*, like the unicorn, was believed to have supernatural powers. In the Middle Ages its crushed root was used to cure the plague. According to the ancient Greeks, the thistle plant protected those who carried it from all harm.

U · The noble *unicorn* has been a mythic figure from time immemorial. Ancient Greeks called him fierce and invincible, vulnerable only to a pure maiden. Centuries later, in the Middle Ages, Christians claimed the unicorn as a symbol of Christ.

V· The *violet* was cultivated in medieval castle gardens for its power over evil spirits, and many were woven into the Unicorn Tapestries. White violets speak of innocence, blue of faithful love. Today a bouquet of violets still means true love.

W · The *Water of Life* can be found in a legendary lake where all good animals come to drink. Once the serpent poisoned the water, but the unicorn dispelled the poison with his ivory horn so that the animals could drink once more.

X · *Xisuthros* was a mythic hero who, like Noah, built an ark. Armenian legend tells of a time when great floods covered the earth, threatening all life. Xisuthros's ark sheltered the animals and sailed to safety with them.

Y. The *yearling unicorn* sleeps beneath the shelter of the *yew tree*. Like the unicorn, the yew is a symbol of immortality. One ancient and revered yew tree is believed to have survived for 2,000 years.

Z · The *zephyr*, a gentle breeze, is the name of the west wind. It blows through the silken mane of the unicorn, who stands upon the zenith gazing down on all creatures of the earth.

Each letter of *The Unicorn Alphabet* is represented by a flower bordering the page. Below is a list of border flowers not mentioned in the text itself:

ASTER In Greek *aster* means "star." Virgil tells us that the aster was used as an altar flower in ancient religious ceremonies.

CARNATION This many-petaled flower was loved for its delicate fragrance. In the fifteenth century it was a popular emblem of betrothal and marriage. In the Gothic Period the carnation was a symbol of rebirth and resurrection.

DAISY This flower, spotless and pure, was a favourite of medieval painters and tapestry weavers. In France it was the flower of Easter, resurrection and rebirth, the flower of spring. In the Middle Ages, German maidens plucked the petals of the daisy one by one, saying, "He loves me, he loves me not. . ." proving that even then this little flower was a measure of love.

ELDERBERRY The berries from this tree can be picked in autumn. Used in many magic spells, the elder is considered the most necromantic tree in the world. Folklore tells us it would be unthinkable for a witch not to have an elder tree in her garden. Quite often, we are told, they actually lived in them. The crushed root of the elder was used to cure the bite of the poisonous adder.

FORGET-ME-NOT French and German poets of the Middle Ages used the image of this delicate blue flower in their love poetry. It is also considered to be a healing herb.

GROUND IVY In the Middle Ages this plant was used in combination with other herbs as an anesthetic. It was also used to ward off the plague, and the leaves were used to relieve the ills of the eyes and ears.

HAWTHORN A beautiful and ancient tree, its flowers have curative powers. From early times its blossoms were used to ease pain and were made into a potion that was applied externally to draw out thorns and splinters.

JONQUIL Also known as the narcissus, this flower is the emblem of chastity and a symbol of Easter and the Resurrection. In folklore it is ascribed the power to ward off evil.

KINGCUP This fair flower blooms in May and was used in May Day festivals as a symbol of fertility. Its presence was believed to ward off danger from witches and evil spirits. A sprig of the kingcup was hung upside down in doorways as protection from evil, and farmers placed it in byres to keep cows from becoming bewitched.

LILY A fragrant and beautiful flower, the lily is the symbol of faithfulness in love and marriage. The lily, like so many other flowers associated with the unicorn, was used against poisonous serpents.

NORTHERN BEDSTRAW In early times this wildflower was used as a rennet to curdle the milk for cheese-making. It is believed to stanch bleeding and heal burns.

ORCHID The root of this wild and exotic purple flower was used by European herbalists in the Middle Ages. The root distilled with wine or milk was drunk as a love potion.

PANSY Known as the "thoughtful flower," the pansy was also called *heartsease*, for it was used to comfort the pains of the heart. Legend tells that a drop of the juice from the pansy in the eye of the one you love will make him or her love you in return.

QUERCUS Latin for *oak*. In the language of love the strong, long-lived oak is an important symbol of fidelity. Its leaves and acorns stand for steadfastness. The oak is also a symbol of military valor and endurance. A powder made from the acorn and bark of the oak was used in herbal medicines as an antitoxin against poison.

STRAWBERRY The fruit was a valuable antidote against all poison and the bite of venomous beasts. This plant, in fruit and flower, is included in countless medieval paintings and tapestries. It was praised for its medicinal properties as well as for its wonderful flavor, which at one time was described as "the food for the blessed."

UNICORN FLOWER Also known as the *starwort*, the root of this ancient medicinal plant was used as a cure for fever, colic, coughs, and in large doses as a mild narcotic.

WALLFLOWER This lemon-colored flower was considered best for medicinal use. A symbol of fertility, it was also believed to ease pain.

XERANTHEMUM This flower was once a symbol of immortality.

YARROW Since ancient times this wild-flowering herb's medicinal virtues have been highly prized. The Greek hero Achilles was said to be advised by the wise centaur Cheiron to use this herb to stanch the wounds of his soldiers.

ZENRY A wild, flowering mustard plant loved by sheep and cattle, the zenry was used as a medicinal plant to heal many ills.